When we speak we are
afraid our words will not
be heard or welcomed.
But when we are silent,
we are still afraid.
So it is better to speak.
—Audre Lorde

We call for the end of
bigotry as we know it. . . . .
We stand for freedom
as we have yet to know it.
And we will not be denied.
—Urvashi Vaid

Big thanks and even bigger love to Lilly Ghahremani
and the OG queer historian Paula Harrowing

Workman Kids
Workman Publishing
Hachette Book Group, Inc.
1290 Avenue of the Americas
New York, NY 10104
workman.com

Workman Kids is an imprint of Workman Publishing, a division of Hachette Book Group, Inc.
The Workman name and logo are registered trademarks of Hachette Book Group, Inc.

Design by Lourdes Ubidia
Cover illustration by Lucy Kirk

The publisher is not responsible for websites (or their content) that are not owned by the publisher.

Workman books may be purchased in bulk for business, educational, or promotional use.
For information, please contact your local bookseller or the Hachette Book Group
Special Markets Department at special.markets@hbgusa.com.

Library of Congress Cataloging-in-Publication Data is available.

ISBN 978-1-5235-1854-8
First Edition April 2024

Distributed in Europe by Hachette Livre, 58 rue Jean Bleuzen, 92 178 Vanves Cedex, France.

Distributed in the United Kingdom by Hachette Book Group,
UK, Carmelite House, 50 Victoria Embankment, London EC4Y 0DZ.

Printed in China on responsibly sourced paper.

10 9 8 7 6 5 4 3 2 1

Contributing Editor
Sachin Bhola

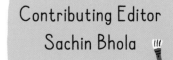

THE ABCs OF QUEER HISTORY

Words by **DR. SEEMA YASMIN**

Pictures by **LUCY KIRK**

WORKMAN PUBLISHING
NEW YORK

A is for **abundant**, because we are many;
our histories show we are diverse and plenty.
From north and south, from here and there,
queer people and queer stories are everywhere!

A is for **always**, for we are not new:
We have been here forever, since the sky has been blue.
We hail from queer **ancestors**, who were here long ago;
we continue their journey, their legacy we grow.

You might be an **ally**, a friend who insists
that every human has the right to exist.
Let's pass on the word, keep our stories **alive**,
and make sure that queer history—like us—will survive.

B is for **belonging**, feeling safe, without fear
in a world that reminds us we're **beloved** and dear.
Being accepted as is and for all that we are
makes us **bold** and empowered. We can sparkle like stars!

B is for **beautiful** words on the page
that speak of our love, our ideas, and our rage.

WE ALL BELONG

There is power in words, in poems and songs;
we find solace in **books**—they make us feel strong.

When we write down our stories, when we tell them aloud,
we invite you to share in what makes us feel proud.
Like Janet Mock said, spread the word, tell these facts,
because sharing queer history is a radical act.

It might take some courage, it might take some heart,
but sharing our lives is a beautiful art.
In the words of **Bayard** Rustin, be fearless, be you,
live your life to the fullest, to your own heart be true.

welcome to our
COMMUNITY GARDEN

LOVE
RULES!

HELP PAINT
THE MURAL

BOOK S

C is for **celebrate**!
Won't you sing this song with me?
I can love who I love, I am free to be me!

D is for **daring**, being authentic and free.
Delight in your life, say: There's no one like me!
To be your full self, don't hide! Look within,
love all that you are, feel at home in your skin.

Dance through the house, on the stage, through the streets;
be inspired by the queer artists you will now meet.
There's Josephine Baker, who shimmied and twirled,
breaking **down** barriers as she **danced** through the world.

Clara Smith sang songs of struggle and cheer,
showing the crowd: Through the pain, we're still here.
They were bisexual women who expressed life through art;
they **demonstrated** courage and danced into our hearts.

Don't forget Chella Man, a **dynamic** pioneer,
fearless in his truth as Asian, **deaf**, and queer.
An actor, an activist, an artist, a star,
like Chella, **dream** big—be all that you are.

E is for **equality**, meaning **each** person on **Earth**
should feel cared for and honored, beginning at birth.
We're fighting for fairness, and it's been a long fight;
queer people, like all, deserve **equal** rights.

E is for **everyone**—leave no person behind.
Open your heart, respect, and be kind.
Pronouns and identities are nothing to fear,
they are letters and words that make ourselves clear.

F is for **family**, both chosen and born,
who love and embrace us—our bond can't be torn.
The families we make or grow into at last
guide us as we travel down life's many paths.

It's not always so easy to see where we belong
when the world seems designed for just one kind of song.
But when we find family who love us from head to toe,
the whole world opens up—love and acceptance we'll know.

Sometimes our **friends** offer strength and support,
like **fantastic** poets Pat Parker and Audre Lorde.
They wrote each other letters to cheer and uplift,
because **friendship** is a blessing, a beautiful gift.

F is for **fluid**, because we change with time:
You don't have to pick labels, you can **fluctuate** like the tides.
Move **freely** through life, explore all you can be!
No need to hold back—**flow** on like the sea.

G

is for **groundbreaking**, like those we hold high:
Innovators who said, the limit's the sky!
From science and music to fashion and arts,
they led by example, with faith in their hearts.

G is for **great**, like Barbara Jordan,
the first queer United States congresswoman.
Although many told her it could never be done,
she believed in herself, she fought, and she won!

MS. JORDAN

G is for **gallant**, like athlete Michael Sam,
who said, "I'm not afraid to tell the world who I am!"
A sportsman at heart, an inspiration to many,
he inspired millions by speaking out bravely.

H is for **hope**, as **Harvey** Milk said:
"Hope will never be silent"; like fire it must be fed.
As an activist and a leader for **human** rights,
Harvey was a politician not scared of a fight.
Though the **hurdles** were many, he strove for justice
and supported a bill to outlaw prejudice.

HOPE WILL NEVER BE SILENT!

I is for **imagination** and the new path ahead.
We create a better world with the words that we spread.
Words like **innovate** and **ideal, include** and **inspire,**
help us lift one another to reach higher and higher.

J is for **joy** that we seek every day
in the memories of loved ones who paved the way.

Like the author **James** Baldwin, who wrote his life on each page,
an honest illustration of queer stories on stage!
And the plays of Lorraine Hansberry, a lesbian writer
who was also an artist, an activist, a fighter.

J is for **jazz**, sounds of rhythm and blues.
Bessie Smith sang with a voice filled with stories and truths.
Tony **Jackson** played piano so the crowds could get down—
they would boogie and spin, smiles emerging from frowns.

K

is for **knowledge**, the power of facts, because **knowing** your truth will help you fight back against hateful old stories and myths that are spread to silence queer people, to hurt and oppress.

Knowing our history means we understand why our identities are feared and our books are banned.
This knowledge is power, it helps us resist:
We can call out the truth and on justice insist.

K is also a call to **keep** your head high, no matter the hate and no matter the lies.
When you know who you are and all that you stand for, you can spread your wings wide and up high you can soar.

L is for **love**, can you spell it with me?
Each **letter** in love is a **lesson**, you'll see!

L is for **liberty**, which means to be free,
because love feels like sailing on warm, open seas.

O is for options, to love who you please;
love means choosing your happiness, living with ease.
V is for vibrant, valued, and venture,
because love is a colorful, precious adventure.
E is for elated, we revel in bliss
when love fills our hearts—there's no feeling like this!

M is for the freedom to **marry** who you please,
a right that was gained after many centuries.
Queer people were treated badly, punished and denied;
they were told their love was wrong, given laws to abide.

Until one day in June the highest court in the land
decided all **marriage** should be celebrated,
no gay marriage banned.

Marriage is a right that we fought for and won,
but don't close your eyes—this fight is not done.

Marriage isn't for everyone, it's not always the goal,
for the sake of justice we shout,
"Marriage equality for all!"

Stand tall, speak up, celebrate each victory,
and keep working together to make history.

N is for **notable,** like the legendary figure
Marsha P. Johnson, whose voice never quivered
when telling the world that all humans are equal,
that we must fight for the rights of transgender people.

And Sylvia Rivera, who was loud and defiant
when transgender people were asked to be quiet.
She said all types of queer people deserve to speak;
together we're strong but divided we're weak.

O is for the **optimists** that we must be,
like Stormé DeLarverie, who said we will be free!
In a suit and bow tie, speaking **openly** and loud,
demanding lesbian rights, she was **out** and proud.

O is for **Osh-Tisch**, who was brave and headstrong
when colonizers said her way of life was wrong.
Invaders insisted Native people change their ways,
but Osh-Tisch practiced her traditions;
she refused to **obey**.

O is for **outspoken**, there are so many we've seen,
like actor George Takei, a legend on screen.
He endured discrimination in its many forms,
but by being himself, stereotypes were transformed.

P is for **Pride**, when we take to the streets.
Come join our **parade**, come follow our beat.
It's a festival, a **party**, we hold hands and sing loud.
We dress in our best, dance, laugh, and feel **proud**!

But Pride is more than one day of the year.
It's being our truest selves and casting out fear.
Pride is waking up every day saying, "I celebrate me."
Pride is looking in the mirror and loving what you see.

Q is for **queens**, of our hearts, of the light—
a glorious tradition. Oh, what a sight!
Strutting on stage, sashay, sashay!
RuPaul is an iconic drag queen who paved the way.

Drag is more than a spectacle, it's more than a scene:
Drag is one way of saying we are here to be seen!
We can dress how we want, different from the rest.
With flair and pizzazz, we turn up as our best.

R is for **reminisce**, **rejoice**, and **renew**,
for the truths of queer lives before me and you.
Never forget the struggles, the hurdles, the fights;
remember their names—in their triumphs delight!

R is for **rock star**!
There's one you must know
for his **remarkable** lyrics,
his **rhythm**, his flow.
Lil Nas X is world-**renowned**;
he **rocks** out on stage till
the crowd is spellbound.
Rock stars and **rebels**,
there are many to **revere**—
we **respect** when they say,
"We're here and we're queer!"

S is for **Stonewall**, the historic protest.
Thousands gathered in the **streets**
with a **simple** request:

Treat queer people with dignity, treat us with respect,
let the laws of the land **safeguard** and protect.

Before that day, a movement had been looming,
but that **summer** morning, there was an uprising.
Police **smashed** into a bar called the **Stonewall Inn**
and confronted the queer patrons partying within.

The Stonewall attack **spurred** queer people to **shout**,
after years of demanding the right to be out.
The battle wasn't new, and it still isn't won,
but Stonewall **signaled** the **start**. A new era had begun.

RiDE

Let us
Love!

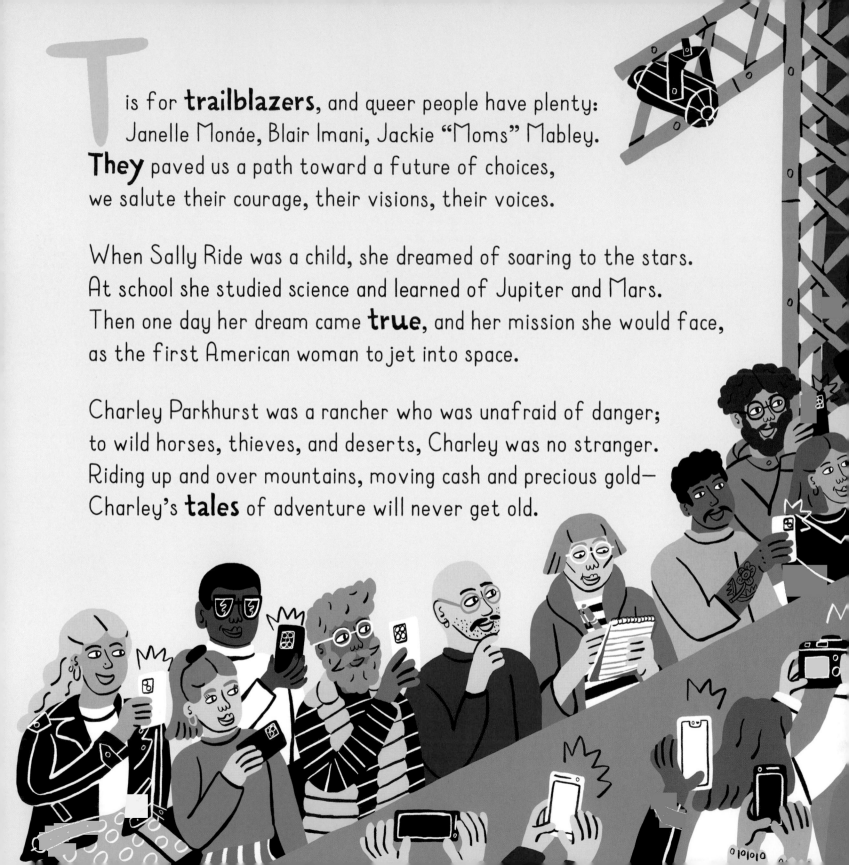

T is for **trailblazers**, and queer people have plenty:
Janelle Monáe, Blair Imani, Jackie "Moms" Mabley.
They paved us a path toward a future of choices,
we salute their courage, their visions, their voices.

When Sally Ride was a child, she dreamed of soaring to the stars.
At school she studied science and learned of Jupiter and Mars.
Then one day her dream came **true**, and her mission she would face,
as the first American woman to jet into space.

Charley Parkhurst was a rancher who was unafraid of danger;
to wild horses, thieves, and deserts, Charley was no stranger.
Riding up and over mountains, moving cash and precious gold—
Charley's **tales** of adventure will never get old.

u is for the ways we **unite** to be strong.
Despite our many differences, we all belong.
Uniting our voices means we're still **unique**!
But we're stronger together, as justice we seek.

Elliot Page says that we must **understand**
to accept one another, so let's join hands.
Uniting means coming together to say,
queer people exist and are here to stay.

When allies join with **us**, we're greater in force,
and we protest together to become one loud voice.
Under one **umbrella**, we march for queer rights;
with respect for our differences, for fairness we fight.

V is for **vital**, as queer people are.
Our contributions help the world and take us far.
Alan Hart was a doctor who found new ways
to help sick people using X-rays.

V is for **vision** to see all that can be,
when we imagine a world where queer people are free.
Vision means learning lessons from the past,
and building a future that's inclusive and **vast**.

W is for **writing** stories and plays,
like Tennessee **Williams**, who gained lots of praise,
including not one but two Pulitzer Prizes,
for tales packed with drama, action, and surprises.

W is for **winning**—what battles we've **won**!
The right to marry, have jobs, to love, and have fun!
But in too many places, sadness hangs in the air,
which is why we must **work** to make the **world** fair.

Wonder to yourself, how can **we** all be free?
What changes can I make? Because change starts with me.

X is for **x-gender**, which comes from Japan,
an identity that is neither woman nor man.

Gender is a spectrum; it's not binary—
you are free to choose your own identity.
Some say this is wrong, that only two options exist,
but as long as we live, this idea we resist.

Nowadays you might hear words like nonbinary,
genderqueer, two-spirit, and GNC—
that stands for gender nonconforming—which is to say:
You don't have to follow, you can make your own way.

Y is for **you** and the choices you make
to live a life of compassion, to learn from mistakes.
You can join our community and march for our rights
because equality is a must—it's everyone's fight.

You have the power to make the world fair.
You can make choices that show that you care.
You can wake up each morning and smile and say,
"I will fight for queer rights, today and every day!"

LOVE

Stonewall Inn

ALLY

...hine Baker

Michael Sam

PROUD

EQUALITY

RESPECT

Chella Man

Barbara Jordan

LGBTQ +

Z is for **zero tolerance**, which means
we won't stand for hatred wherever it's seen.
There's no room for prejudice, homophobia, or bias.
We should all be valued; respect should be highest.

Z is for a **zillion** queer stories, as old as the Earth!
In your hands is one droplet; there's much more to learn.
An ocean of stories, a galaxy of sagas,
wisdom and adventure, escapades and drama.

Z is for **zeal,** of which you have plenty,
to share all you know about these queer histories.
So go into the world and share these stories—
tales of hope and activism, tales of legends and glory.

The ABCs of Queer History: Terms and Figures

Queer history is packed full of icons, legends, and trailblazers—including musicians, artists, doctors, athletes, and activists. Many of them rose up against injustice so that all queer people could live their lives safely and freely. Queer history is full of words and phrases that have come and gone and shifted with the times. There's simply too much queer history and language to include in one book, but here are more details on the people and phrases you've just read about.

LGBTQIA+ stands for lesbian, gay, bisexual, transgender, queer or questioning, intersex, and asexual or aromantic. The + sign means it also includes people who might identify in different ways—we don't want to leave anybody out! LGBTQIA+ aims to include all the ways people think about their gender and sexuality. Sexuality is the way people describe their feelings toward other people. These feelings can be emotional feelings like love, or physical and sexual feelings such as being attracted to another person.

Let's break down the terms. People who are attracted to others of the same gender are "gay." "Lesbian" is often used if they are women. (Those attracted to someone of a different gender are "straight" or "heterosexual.") "Bisexual" or "pansexual" refers to being attracted to people regardless of gender (more on gender in the next column). "Queer" can refer to people who do not identify as straight. People who are questioning their sexuality or gender identity may not have decided how they define themselves or may not want to label themselves. Intersex people have body parts that don't easily fit into the categories of male or female. Someone who is "asexual" may not experience sexual attraction at all, and "aromantic" people don't experience romantic attraction.

The Black feminist author bell hooks thought of queerness "not as being about who you're having sex with—that can be a dimension of it—but queer as being about the self that is at odds with everything around it and it has to invent and create and find a place to speak and to thrive and to live."

Gender and Sex

Gender and sex are two different things that often get mixed up. Sex has to do with what a person's body looks like and what it can do (it's mostly focused on the organs that can make and support a baby, such as a uterus, breasts, or a penis) and what kinds of chromosomes (long strings of genes) are inside their cells. Gender is different. Gender is a social construct, an idea we invent and reinvent. Race is another social construct that was invented by some people to classify and categorize humans, and allow some to have more power and control than others. Gender is not fixed. Gender is shaped by historical, cultural, and social factors.

Even though race and gender are socially constructed, they are very powerful. In our society, the way people are treated relies very much on rules about gender norms. Most people who follow these old rules think about gender as having only two options: You can either be a boy or a girl. This system with only two options is called the gender binary. People like Chella Man who are genderqueer, nonbinary, or gender nonconforming believe there are *many* more ways to think about and express gender. They certainly feel there are more than just two options! When we live in a society that mostly still thinks about gender in a narrow, binary way, it can be helpful to use the terms AFAB and AMAB. These stand for "assigned female at birth" and "assigned male at birth." They refer to the way people, including doctors, quickly decide a baby's gender based on what the baby's outside organs look like.

A transgender person is someone whose gender identity does not correspond with the sex they were assigned at birth. So a trans man might have been AFAB but now lives life as a man. At birth, people might have been referred to with the pronouns she/her/hers, but now they might use the pronouns he/him/his. Trans people can also be gender nonconforming and choose gender neutral pronouns like they/them/theirs.

Audre Lorde (1934-1992)

Audre Lorde was everything. A self-described "Black, lesbian, mother, warrior, poet," she was also a professor, a librarian, and a role model to many. Beloved for her poetry and memoirs, Lorde invented a new way of writing stories about ourselves called "biomythography," which mixes autobiography, history, and myth.

Urvashi Vaid (1958-2022)

Urvashi Vaid was an Indian-born American-based lawyer, lesbian, and LGBTQIA+ activist. She was tireless and outspoken in her fight for equality. At the height of the HIV/AIDS crisis, Vaid led the National LGBTQ Task Force and pushed for access to medications for all people living with the virus.

A is for Abundant, Always, Ally

Queer people have been around for as long as humans have walked the planet, even if the names we call ourselves and the words we use to describe queerness have changed. Abundance means there are many of us, although, to this day, many queer people feel unsafe to be themselves because of anti-queer prejudice and laws that make being queer a crime.

An ally to queer people is someone who supports the rights of queer people to live freely. Some say "'ally' is a verb, not a noun," meaning it's what you *do* to support equal rights that really counts—simply calling yourself an ally is not enough.

B is for Belonging, Beautiful, Books, Bigotry, Bayard Rustin

Belonging is important to humans because it helps us feel safe and connected to others. We feel we belong when we are around people who accept us for all that we are. Books are one medium that has helped queer people find belonging throughout history, especially when the stories on the page reflect our lives.

Janet Mock is one of the first Black trans women to write a network TV show in the United States. Born in Hawaii, Mock is a director, bestselling author, and transgender rights activist.

Bayard Rustin (1912–1987) was a Black, gay civil rights activist who helped organize the 1963 March on Washington for Jobs and Freedom. That was the march at which Dr. Martin Luther King Jr. gave his famous "I Have a Dream" speech. What's less well-known about that march is that it would not have happened without Rustin's efforts. In less than two months, he organized the largest demonstration ever seen in the United States—more than a quarter of a million people gathered in Washington that day. But because of society's hatred toward gay people, Rustin was often denied the credit he deserved. In fact, he was arrested in 1953 for breaking a law that targeted queer people. He was only pardoned for that "crime" in 2020, 37 years after his death. In 2013, 50 years after the march, President Barack Obama awarded Rustin the Presidential Medal of Freedom for his important role in organizing the historic event.

Bigotry is hatred toward people because they belong to a particular group. When bigotry is directed toward gay people, it's called homophobia, and when it's targeted toward all queer people, it's called queerphobia.

C is for Celebrate

Queer history includes many dark chapters. To this day, bigoted politicians write laws that make it a crime to be queer. Some people are shunned by their families because they are queer. Amid this pain, it's important that we remember two things: First, queer people have been—and continue to be—punished just for being who we are; and second, look at how far we've come! Queer history is resplendent with stories of love, joy, freedom, and creativity. Queer contributions to society are many. It was likely a queer woman, **Maude Russell Rutherford (1897–2001)**, who invented the famous Charleston dance. It was a drag artist, **Paris Dupree (1950–2011)**, who invented a style of dance known as voguing, which became mainstream when straight artists copied the moves. It was a queer woman, **Dr. Sara Josephine Baker (1873–1945)**, who invented a way to prevent babies from losing their sight.

D is for Daring, Dance, Deaf

Josephine Baker (1906–1975) was a Black, bisexual woman who was a dancer, actress, singer, civil rights activist, and World War II spy. Baker was born and raised in the United States but moved to France because of racist laws that kept Black Americans separate from White Americans. Baker's influence on dance and music, including her famous banana skirt, are still present today.

Clara Smith (1894–1935) was a Black, bisexual blues singer, nicknamed "Queen of the Moaners" because of her sultry voice. Smith and Baker were friends and likely partners. Today, we use the words "bisexual" or "queer" to describe them, but in the early 1900s, different words and phrases were used to describe women who love women. One of these terms was "lady lover."

Baker and Smith were two of *many* Black, queer blues singers, dancers, and entertainers of that time. Others include **Gladys Bentley (1907–1960)**, **Alberta Hunter (1895–1984)**, **Ma Rainey (1886–1939)**, **Bessie Smith (1894–1937)**, **Ethel Waters (1886–1977)**, **Billie Holiday (1915–1959)**, and **Lucille Bogan (1897–1948)**. Some, such as Hunter, were closeted, meaning they mostly didn't talk about their queerness with people they didn't know. Some, such as Bogan and Holiday, were out, meaning they were open about their sexuality. Gladys Bentley was an out lesbian. She often dressed in masculine clothes and flirted with women while she sang, and was sometimes promoted as a male impersonator. Bentley told a gossip columnist that she was married. When the columnist asked: "Well, who's the man?" Bentley said: "Man? It's a woman."

Chella Man (1998–) is a Jewish, Chinese, deaf artist, author, YouTuber, LGBTQIA+ activist, and director. Man is genderqueer and nonbinary, two words that describe a person whose gender does not fit into the usual categories of man or woman.

Baker, Bessie Smith, and Man—and everyone who is honest about what gender really is—are daring individuals. They boldly live their lives and express themselves according to their wishes.

E is for Equality

Equality means that no one is left out and everyone is treated fairly. Unfortunately, throughout history and to this day, disabled people, darker-skinned people, and queer people, among others, are not given the same respect as nondisabled, White, straight people. There are many other reasons that a person might be treated unequally. Striving for equality means we want to create a world where everyone is treated with compassion and kindness, no matter what they look like, how much money they have, how they talk, or who they love—no matter what.

F is for Family, Friendship

Family is the group of people with whom you feel you truly belong. For queer people, family might look like a mix of those who are biological relatives and others with whom we have found true kinship. Friendship is essential to the happiness and even survival of many queer people. Friends who love, accept, challenge, and encourage us are precious. Poets **Pat Parker (1944–1989)** and **Audre Lorde (1934–1992)** had a beautiful friendship. They wrote each other letters of support and inspiration. "I have always loved you, Pat, and wanted for you those things you wanted deeply for yourself," wrote Lorde in a 1985 letter to Parker.

The **Ballroom Scene** is a queer Black and Latine subculture that was created in New York City in the 1970s. In the Ballroom Scene, also known as ball culture, people perform in dance and fashion shows. Groups of performers band together into "houses" that become their chosen families. Each house has a "mother" and "father," who are usually older and more experienced people who look out for the younger, newer members. Some performers find true family in the Ballroom Scene.

G is for Groundbreaking, Great, Gallant

When someone is creative, comes up with new ideas, or is the first to achieve something, we say they are groundbreaking.

"Gallant" means brave and courageous. **Barbara Charline Jordan (1936–1996)** and **Michael Alan Sam Jr. (1990–)** are examples of gallant and groundbreaking queer people. Jordan achieved many firsts: She was the first Black person elected to the Texas Senate, the first Black woman from the South to join the United States House of Representatives, the first woman to ever give the keynote speech at the Democratic National Convention, and the first Black woman to be buried in the Texas State Cemetery. Jordan was open about her sexuality with those close to her but never publicly came out as queer. Her life partner of nearly 30 years was Nancy Earl.

Sam became the first openly gay football player to be drafted by a National Football League team in 2014.

H is for Hope, Harvey Milk

In 1977, **Harvey Milk (1930–1978)** became one of the first openly gay men to be elected to public office in the United States and the first to be elected in California. Milk believed that if queer people were elected to positions where they could help write and pass laws, they could create real change and make equality truly possible. He was determined to use his position on the San Francisco Board of Supervisors to make the city safer and cleaner. Milk spearheaded a law that would make it illegal to discriminate against queer people. At the time, queer people could be refused a safe place to live, treated badly at work, or even refused a job, just because they were not straight—and this kind of discrimination wasn't considered a crime. On June 25, 1978 (the 10th anniversary of the Stonewall protests—more on Stonewall under "S"), Milk gave a speech on the steps of San Francisco's City Hall that came to be known as "the Hope speech." Milk fought tirelessly for gay rights and worked hard to get lawmakers on his side to support the new law.

The line "hope will never be silent" may not have been uttered directly by Milk, but it sums up his message of righteous anger at the way queer people were treated and the need to imagine a better future. "Hope will never be silent" has become a famous tagline inspired by Milk that you will find on paintings, T-shirts, and artwork bearing his face.

I is for Imagination, Innovate, Include

Queer people have been discriminated against throughout history—but we continue to imagine a world where everyone is free. If you work each day to make this world a reality, you are innovating, meaning you are inventing a better future.

J is for Joy, Jazz, James Baldwin

James Arthur Baldwin (1924–1987) was an iconic author and thinker. He wrote poems, novels, memoirs, and plays, and spoke openly about what it was like to be a Black gay man in a racist and homophobic country. He was born in Harlem, New York, and like Josephine Baker, moved to France because he felt freer to be himself there. For many years, some people talked about Baldwin's work without mentioning that he was a gay man even though Baldwin wrote about queer life and relationships between men in his books.

Lorraine Hansberry (1930–1965) was a playwright from Chicago who wrote the famous play *A Raisin in the Sun*. The play tells the story of Black Americans in Chicago who face racism. Hansberry was a member of the Daughters of Bilitis, one of America's first lesbian organizations.

Jazz is a style of music that was pioneered by Black Americans. Jazz mixes gospel, the blues, African rhythms, and other styles of music to create a sound that can fill you with joy. Some of the most popular jazz music was created and performed by queer artists.

Bessie Smith (1894–1937), also known as the "Empress of the Blues," was a popular Black blues and jazz singer who was born in Tennessee. Black entertainers did not have many chances to make a career because of extreme anti-Black racism in the United States. One of the few opportunities they had was with traveling troupes of Black performers who went from town to town singing, dancing, and performing stand-up comedy in tents.

When she was in her late twenties, Smith married a man named Jack Gee. She often had relationships with women and sang about her love of women in her songs.

Tony Jackson (1876–1921) was an openly gay Black man who was born into a poor family in New Orleans. When he was only 10 years old, Jackson made a harpsichord out of junk and used it to play hymns. He rose to fame as a talented jazz pianist but left New Orleans for Chicago because it was considered a safer place to be a Black man at the time. Jackson wrote a song called "Pretty Baby" in 1916. Some say the original lyrics were about his lover man, but when the song was performed by other musicians, they rewrote the lyrics.

K is for Knowledge, Keep

Knowledge is the antidote to lies. When people make up bad stories about queer people, you can push back with knowledge. Knowledge about the diversity of queer history. Knowledge about the contributions queer people have made to society. Knowledge that reminds you that no one is free until we are all free.

L is for Love

There are many different types of love. Loving and being loved are essential to our health and well-being. For centuries, queer people have loved one another even beneath the dark shadows of bigotry and prejudice. Love fuels queer people and their allies to fight for equality and justice.

M is for Marriage

Marriage is when people come together and agree to love and care for each other. Marriage is a legal act, which means there are rules about who can get married. These rules are different around the world. For many years in the United States, marriage was only allowed between a man and a woman. After years of fighting for the equal right to get married, marriage between two men or two women was made legal in the United States in 2015. Most countries don't allow gay marriage, but the list of countries that do is growing. Some politicians in the U.S. are trying to make gay marriage illegal again, so this fight is far from over.

N is for Notable

Notable people are remarkable and outstanding for how they lived their lives and all they achieved. **Marsha "Pay It No Mind" Johnson (1945–1992)** was a Black activist and drag mother who fought hard for all queer people to be treated equally. As a child, Marsha felt happy and like her true self when she wore clothes designed for women, but she stopped because she was harassed and physically attacked. Nowadays, we use the word "transgender" to describe Johnson, but when she was alive, that term wasn't as common. Johnson used words such as "transvestite," "drag queen," and "gay" to describe herself, and she used she/her pronouns. Johnson is remembered for playing an important part as a protestor in the historic Stonewall uprising of 1969.

Sylvia Rivera (1951–2002) was a close friend of Marsha P. Johnson. She was also transgender, a queer rights activist, and a woman of color. Like Johnson, Rivera was bullied and attacked for being different when she was a young child. The bullying was so bad that she ran away from home when she was 11 years old. Rivera met Johnson, and later said, "She was like a mother to me."

Rivera played an important role in the history of queer rights. Some people said that it was Rivera who threw the first exploding weapon at police during the Stonewall Inn protests, but in 2001, Rivera said she threw the second.

After the protest, when gay organizations continued advocating for queer people but ignored the work that trans people had done, Rivera would not stand for it. She wanted the world to know that trans people were central to the fight for equality.

Marsha P. Johnson & Sylvia Rivera

O is for Optimists, Outspoken

Optimists are full of hope. Outspoken optimists help us all imagine a future that is freer and fairer than the world we live in now.

Stormé DeLarverie (1920–2014) was born in New Orleans to a Black mother and a White father. DeLarverie began singing songs, sometimes dressed as a woman and sometimes as a man. She made a name for herself when she left New Orleans and moved to Chicago, where she joined the Jewel Box Revue, a group of female impersonators who traveled the country putting on shows. DeLarverie was the only member of the Revue who dressed and performed as a man.

The words we use to describe people change over the years. Some have said that DeLarverie was a butch lesbian ("butch" means to dress and behave in a masculine way). Some have described her as genderfluid or as a cross-dresser. DeLarverie became even more famous in 1969 during the Stonewall Inn protests. There was a rumor that she was the first person at the Inn to punch a police officer, and while it was never proven, DeLarverie insisted it was true.

Osh-Tisch (1854–1929) was a warrior and leader from the Apsáalooke tribe who lived in the area that we now call Montana. The Apsáalooke are also known as the Crow people. Osh-Tisch lived life doing things that were considered stereotypically masculine *and* feminine. For example, Osh-Tisch was a brave and skilled fighter (which people might say is a traditionally masculine role) and good at sewing (which some might say is a traditionally feminine activity). People like Osh-Tisch are called "baté" in the Apsáalooke language. Among the Apsáalooke, baté are highly respected. Unfortunately, the White colonizers who killed many Indigenous people and stole their land did not like the Apsáalooke's way of life. They wanted everyone to be straight and to act like either a man or a woman. In the late 1890s, White colonizers said that being baté was wrong. They tried to force all baté to act as stereotypical men, meaning they could be warriors but could not do things like sew. Osh-Tisch's elder, Chief Pretty Eagle, was outspoken and defended the baté. Sadly, Osh-Tisch is believed to be one of the last baté of that time.

Beginning in the 1990s, Indigenous activists used a new word to describe the many systems of gender classification among their cultures. That word is "two-spirit." Don't confuse "two-spirit" with "transgender." "Two-spirit" is a uniquely Indigenous word. It's an umbrella term that's used to talk about many of the ways Indigenous Americans think about gender that don't fit into the binary system. However, each nation has its own ideas about gender and unique words to describe these ideas.

George Takei (1937–) is a gay, Japanese American actor and activist who is most famous for starring in the TV series *Star Trek*. When he was a young boy, Takei and his family were put in a prison camp for being Japanese American. At the time, the United States was at war with Japan, and the government said that Japanese American people were dangerous. Living through this injustice and seeing his parents treated badly encouraged Takei to become an activist fighting for an end to racism. But for many years, Takei did not speak out about being gay. He said he felt he had to hide who he was because of the homophobia in Hollywood. "I learned at a young age that you couldn't be an openly gay actor and hope to be employed," he said. "And I was already an Asian American actor, so I was already limited a lot."

Takei came out as a gay man when he was 68 years old. He did this because he was angry that Arnold Schwarzenegger, the governor of California at the time, was refusing to make gay marriage legal. At the time, Takei had been with his partner, Brad Altman, for 18 years. The couple got married in 2008, four months after gay marriage was made legal in California.

P is for Pride

Pride means feeling happy about something you have achieved or feeling pleased with who you are. Gay Pride is a celebration of queer history and queer people past and present. Gay Pride parades feature music, floats, and people walking and dancing. Some countries celebrate a gay Pride day or month, and there are gay Pride celebrations all around the world.

Q is for Queens

Gender is a made-up set of rules and ideas about how people should act. The idea of what a boy does and what a boy looks like are rules created by society. Drag performers play with these rules by amping up the performance of gender: Drag queens and kings exaggerate what it means to be feminine and masculine. Drag plays outside of the gender binary. But drag is so much more than makeup, music, and a show. Drag is a way queer people have expressed themselves and taken a stand against society's narrow rules. Drag has also allowed people to be visibly queer in a society that often wants us to be invisible and ashamed.

There are many legendary drag performers. **Dred (1971–2019)** was a Haitian American drag king who rose to fame in New York City in the 1990s. **Lady Bunny (1962–)** is an iconic drag queen from Tennessee who founded Wigstock in 1984. Wigstock is an outdoor drag festival that takes place almost every year. **RuPaul Andre Charles (1960–)** is a drag queen, actor, and TV show host who began to perform in drag when he was in his twenties. He is one of the most famous drag queens in the world and has starred in movies and his own TV show, *RuPaul's Drag Race*.

R is for Reminisce, Rejoice, Renew, Rock Stars, Remarkable, Rebels

A remarkable person is someone who's special and impressive. That certainly describes **Lil Nas X (1999–)**, a Black rapper and songwriter from Georgia. In 2019, the performer came out as gay and is now one of the most high-profile openly gay rappers.

S is for Stonewall, Safeguard, Spurred

The **Stonewall Inn** is a bar in Manhattan's West Village that felt like a safe space to be queer at a time when police could arrest queer people for gathering together or for dressing in ways that did not conform to gender norms. On June 28, 1969, police ran into the Inn and began to attack the queer people inside. This fight sparked a protest that lasted five days, with queer people marching for the right to be treated with decency and respect. Queer people had been speaking out for equal rights for decades. The protests spurred even more people to join the fight for equal rights.

T is for Trailblazers

People who pave the way, share new ideas, and inspire us are called trailblazers. Here are just a few queer trailblazers, past and present.

Janelle Monáe (1985–) is a Black singer, author, and actress from Kansas. Monáe has been nominated for eight Grammy awards. She is pansexual and nonbinary.

Blair Imani (1993–) is a queer, Black, bisexual Muslim educator, historian, and activist. Imani went viral in 2016 when she was photographed while being arrested by police for protesting the racist killing of Alton Sterling in Louisiana.

Jackie "Moms" Mabley (1894–1975) was a comedian and actress from North Carolina who was known as the funniest woman in the world. As a Black woman who came out as a lesbian in 1921, Mabley fought through racism, sexism, and homophobia to become a successful performer.

Sally Ride (1951–2012) was a White American astronaut from California who jetted into space at the age of 32. She kept her nearly 30-year-long relationship with a woman a secret from the public.

Charley Parkhurst (1812–1879) was one of the best horse and stagecoach drivers in the West. Trusted by banks to transport gold across dangerous lands, Parkhurst, who'd had one of his eyes kicked out by a horse, was seen as brave and fierce. It was only after his death that the legendary stagecoach driver was discovered to have been assigned female at birth.

U is for Unite, Unique, Understand

Being united means joining together so no one feels alone. Our voices are louder and we are all stronger when we stand together to fight for justice. But being in a group doesn't mean you have to be like everyone else. You can be unique, which means being different and being yourself. When we accept other people's differences, we are showing that we understand that we can be ourselves while coming together to seek equality.

Elliot Page (1987–) is a White, Oscar-nominated, Canadian actor who came out as a transgender man in 2020. He says being his true self has made him very happy. Page wrote in *Esquire* magazine, "What have I learned from transitioning? I can't overstate the biggest joy, which is really seeing yourself. I know I look different to others, but to me I'm just starting to look like myself. It's indescribable, because I'm just like, there I am."

V is for Vital, Vision, Vast

Queer icons who see a future where all people are free have been central in the fight for queer rights. Their vision has been vital—meaning important—to help everyone imagine what is possible. Back when **Alan L. Hart (1890–1962)** was a doctor, the illness tuberculosis was hard to detect. But Hart, who was a radiologist (an expert in using X-rays to diagnose disease), discovered that chest X-rays could help tuberculosis patients learn what was wrong with them and get help early on, before they became dangerously sick. Hart was born in Kansas, and lived most of his adult life as what we would now call a transgender man. Hart's work has saved millions of lives—to this day, we still use Hart's discovery to help people who are sick with tuberculosis get the help they need as early as possible.

W is for Writing, Winning, Wonder, We, Tennessee Williams

Brave writers have helped us understand queer life over the decades and around the world, including queer writers who were jailed for writing queer stories. **Tennessee Williams**

(1911–1983) was a White, gay man and one of America's most famous and celebrated playwrights. He won a Pulitzer Prize for his play *A Streetcar Named Desire* in 1948, and a second Pulitzer for his play *Cat on a Hot Tin Roof* in 1955. Williams was an openly gay man at a time when it was not easy to be out. He included gay characters in his plays.

X is for X-gender

Many Western societies use a gender binary that limits people to one of two options: You're either a boy or a girl. But in Japanese culture, the term "x-gender" (Xジェンダー in Japanese) is used to describe someone who is neither or both. It's used in a similar way to the English terms "genderqueer," "gender nonconforming," and "nonbinary." X-gender people in Japan sometimes use the same Pride flag as nonbinary people.

Y is for You

Yes, you! Whether you are queer, questioning, or an ally, each one of you can make a change in the world. How will you make the world better? Will you ask questions about why things are the way they are? Will you treat every single person with equal care and respect? There are so many ways that you can help to build a future in which queer people are free.

Z is for Zero Tolerance, Zillion, Zeal

The zero tolerance approach means that we call out homophobia when we see it (when it's safe for us to do so) and that we live our lives in a way that shows respect and kindness to all people.

There are a zillion ways to do this, just as there are a zillion ways to be queer, questioning, or an ally.

Whatever you do to be inclusive and kind, do it with zeal! That means being enthusiastic and passionate about creating a world in which queer stories are shared, celebrated, and continue to be lived!

SEEMA YASMIN

Seema Yasmin is a medical doctor, author, and Emmy Award–winning journalist. Her books paint vivid pictures about ourselves and how we interact with the world around us. They include *What the Fact?!: Finding the Truth in All the Noise, Muslim Women Are Everything*, the poetry collection *If God Is a Virus*, and more. Please visit SeemaYasmin.com.

LUCY KIRK

Lucy Kirk is a freelance illustrator and ceramist based in Bristol, UK. Since graduating from Brighton University in 2012, she has worked with a wide range of different clients and varied projects. These include editorial illustrations, book illustrations, print and pattern designs, murals, fashion, and ceramic designs. Her work is playful and refreshing with an edgy humor.